This book is presented to

_____

by_____

on_____

For Benjamin, Timothy, Miriam, and Sarah,
for whom this book was written.

Published by Concordia Publishing House
3558 S. Jefferson Avenue, St. Louis, MO 63118-3968
1-800-325-3040 • www.cph.org

Text © 2014 by Ruth M. Meyer

Illustrations © 2014 Concordia Publishing House

Manufactured in Heshan,China/047365/300502

1 2 3 4 5 6 7 8 9 10   23 22 21 20 19 18 17 16 15 14

OUR
FAITH
FROM
A TO Z

Ruth M. Meyer
Illustrated by Dave Hill

CONCORDIA PUBLISHING HOUSE • SAINT LOUIS

A is for **Apostles' Creed**, written long ago
To simply state what we believe, that we in faith may grow.

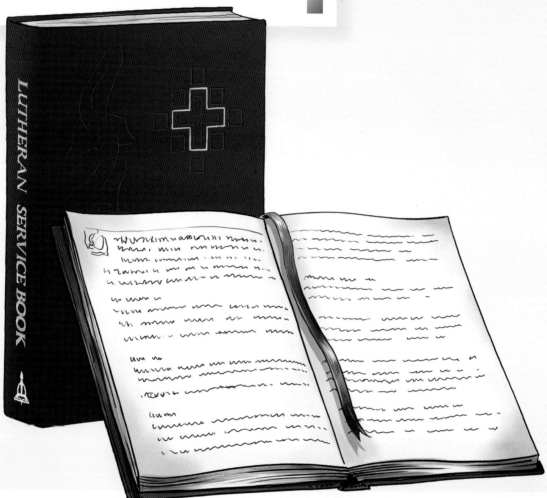

Apostles' Creed: The word "creed" comes from the Latin word *credo*, which means "I believe." As Lutherans, we confess three ecumenical, or universal, creeds: the Apostles' Creed, the Nicene Creed, and the Athanasian Creed. Many Christians all over the world confess these creeds. The Apostles' Creed is the oldest of the three. It briefly states our beliefs as taught in the Bible. There are three sections, or "articles," in the Apostles' Creed, each of which focuses on one person of the Holy Trinity. The First Article describes the work of God the Father, the Creator of all things. The Second Article describes the work of the Second Person of the Holy Trinity, Jesus. This article focuses on the work of redemption, or salvation, which Jesus accomplished for us by His death and resurrection. The Third Article of the Apostles' Creed directs us to God the Holy Spirit, who sanctifies us, or makes us holy. We confess this creed or the Nicene Creed together in church every week as a declaration of our beliefs.

In **Baptism**, our letter **B**, a miracle takes place. As God's Word and water makes you a child of God by grace.

Baptism: Baptism is a sacrament. A sacrament is a saving gift that is instituted (begun) by God, combines God's Word with a visible element, and gives the forgiveness of sins. Jesus Himself instituted Holy Baptism by commanding His disciples to "go . . . and make disciples of all nations, baptizing them in the name of the Father and of the Son and of the Holy Spirit" (Matthew 28:19). When someone is baptized, the pastor baptizes him or her in the name of the Triune God. While doing so, the pastor pours water, the visible element, on the head of the person receiving Baptism. Baptism has tremendous power. Because of the Word and promises of God, Baptism works forgiveness of sins and grants eternal salvation. Many Lutherans were baptized as babies. We believe that infants are included in God's command to baptize "all nations." Likewise, we believe that we are all born sinful and therefore need God's forgiveness. The promises of Baptism apply to babies, children, and adults alike. For babies and children, the tradition of assigning godparents, or sponsors, helps encourage the baptized child to continue in his or her God-given faith.

Catechism
is our

C,

written for
our gain,
   As Luther
wrote of
Six Chief
Parts, the
Scriptures
to explain. ■

LUTHER'S
SMALL
CATECHISM

Catechism: Martin Luther wrote his Small Catechism in 1529 as a way to teach the Christian faith. He wrote questions and answers for the Six Chief Parts of the catechism: the Ten Commandments, the Apostles' Creed, the Lord's Prayer, Baptism, Confession, and Communion (the Sacrament of the Altar). Luther also included daily prayers and a table of duties for Christians in their various walks of life. The Small Catechism is a summary of what the Bible teaches, and it is taught to students before they are confirmed. Confirmation is a rite in which individuals "confirm" that they know and believe what the Church teaches and are ready for full membership in the congregation. Confirmands—students who are preparing for confirmation—are usually required to memorize the catechism. Families are encouraged to use the catechism in devotional time together, and all Christians are encouraged to learn it by heart. Luther himself envisioned families teaching these words to their children. He encourages us in the Small Catechism preface to "teach [the children] first of all the Ten Commandments, the Creed, the Lord's Prayer, et cetera, according to the text, word for word, so that they can repeat it after you and commit it to memory."

D now stands for **Doctrine**, teachings we hold dear.
We take them strictly from God's Word,
where He has made them clear.

LARGE CATECHISM

APOLOGY (DEFENSE) OF
THE AUGSBURG CONFESSION

THE FORMULA OF CONCORD

SMALL CATECHISM

AUGSBURG CONFESSION

THE HOLY BIBLE

Doctrine: The word "doctrine" means "teaching." In this context, doctrine includes the entire set of beliefs we hold as Lutherans. Our church fathers confess, as do we, that "God's Word alone should be and remain the only standard and rule of doctrine" (Formula of Concord Solid Declaration, Rule and Norm, 9). In other words, we teach what the Bible teaches. We do not make up beliefs or change what the Bible says in any way. The Book of Concord compiles writings from the Lutheran church fathers that state for the record what Lutheran doctrine is. The writings include the Small and Large Catechisms, the Augsburg Confession, the Apology (Defense) of the Augsburg Confession, the Formula of Concord, and other writings that explain our doctrine. The Bible is our only authority because it is the actual Word of God. Our teachings as laid out in the Book of Concord are in complete doctrinal agreement with the Bible, and so serve as a standard in Lutheranism to determine faithful biblical teaching.

Evangelism
is our

E.

God wants His Church to grow,

So we go forth to share God's love, that all the world may know.

Evangelism: Evangelism is simply sharing our faith with other people. Jesus tells us in Matthew 28:19–20, "Go therefore and make disciples of all nations, baptizing them in the name of the Father and of the Son and of the Holy Spirit, and teaching them to observe all that I have commanded you." Jesus wants us to tell other people about Him! We can invite a friend to go to church and Sunday School with us, talk about Jesus with him or her, say a prayer with him or her before we eat, and live our lives in a way that shows we are Christian. If anyone asks us why we are Christians or what a Christian believes, we can say this: Everyone on earth is a sinner and does bad things. Jesus, God's Son, came to earth as a human. He lived a perfect life for us, and then He was crucified, or put to death on a cross, for our sins. He took upon Himself the punishment we sinners deserve. After three days, He rose again from the dead. He has victory over death! Because of Jesus, we will not be punished eternally for our sins. Whoever believes in Jesus will someday live with Him forever in heaven. That news is too good not to share!

"Faith alone" brings us to

F,

a teaching we maintain.

Our works can't save; only Christ can heaven for us gain. ∎

Faith Alone: The doctrine of justification through "faith alone" by "grace alone" on account of "Christ alone" is the most important teaching in the Bible. Ephesians 2:8–9 is very clear: "For by grace you have been saved through faith. And this is not your own doing; it is the gift of God, not a result of works, so that no one may boast." This emphasizes that Jesus is the only way to heaven. He is one hundred percent responsible for our salvation. We gain heaven through faith in Him, and this is only by His grace. We cannot earn heaven by being a "good" person.

God demands perfection, and we are all sinners who deserve eternal punishment. By God's grace, Jesus is the answer to God's demands for a perfect life. Jesus has done everything needed for us to enter heaven; we do not need to do anything else. All other religions teach that a person has to do enough good works to earn their way to heaven. Even some other Christian denominations teach that we have to contribute something to our own salvation. We, as Lutherans, teach that Jesus has done everything already. All the credit and glory goes to Christ!

The Bible tells us who **God** is, and this is letter

G.

He's Father, Son, and Holy Ghost: the Holy Trinity.

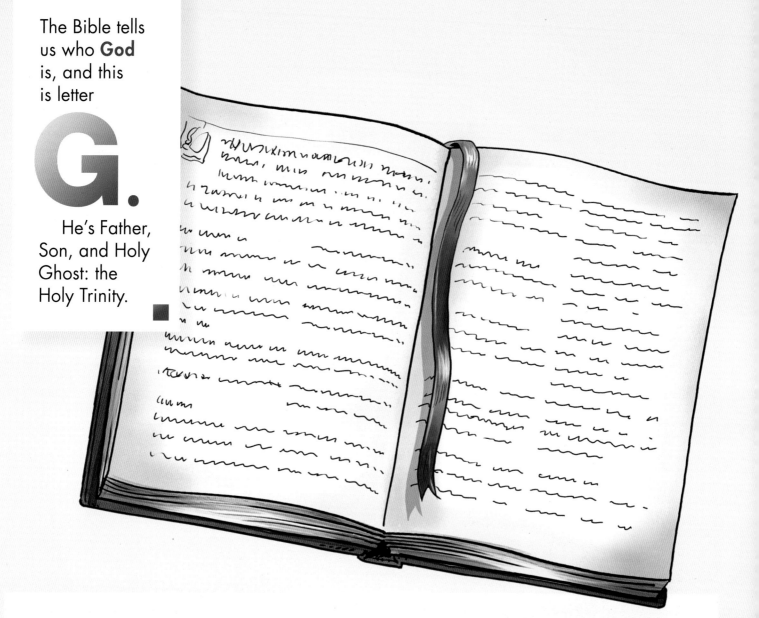

God: Who is God? We, as Lutherans, confess the one true God as revealed in the Bible. He is one God in three persons: God the Father, God the Son, and God the Holy Spirit—the Holy Trinity. The Bible clearly states that there is only one God. Deuteronomy 6:4 tells us, "Hear, O Israel: the LORD our God, the LORD is one." We do not believe in three gods. At the same time, Jesus instructs us to baptize "in the name of the Father and of the Son and of the Holy Spirit" (Matthew 28:19), teaching us that there is one God in three persons. The apostle Paul also affirms the teaching of the Trinity in 2 Corinthians 13:14, where he gives a blessing: "The grace of the Lord Jesus Christ and the love of God and the fellowship of the Holy Spirit be with you all." The Athanasian Creed was specifically written to defend and explain our belief in the Trinity. Our minds cannot fully understand this truth, but God Himself tells us it is so, and we believe it. As an example, some people use an apple. The apple has a core, the white part inside (the flesh), and the skin. Each of these parts has its own purpose, and yet it is one apple. So it is with the Holy Trinity. As we sing in the hymn "Holy, Holy, Holy," "God in three persons, blessed Trinity!" (*LSB* 507:1).

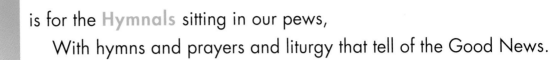

H is for the **Hymnals** sitting in our pews,
With hymns and prayers and liturgy that tell of the Good News.

Hymnals: Our hymnals are valuable resources for our Lutheran worship services. Although other hymnals are available, many congregations now use the *Lutheran Service Book*. The *Lutheran Service Book* contains psalms from the Bible, which we use during our church services, as well as settings for the Divine Service and other orders of worship. It also includes prayers, the Small Catechism, and Bible reading plans. The largest section is made up of the hymns we sing in church. There are more than six hundred hymns, arranged topically. There are hymns for the different seasons of the Church Year—Advent, Christmas, Epiphany, and so on—as well as hymns that deal with specific topics. The *Lutheran Service Book* includes hymns about justification, sanctification, trust, prayer, praise, and many others. We use these hymns, orders of service, psalms, and prayers in our worship services every week.

is **Invocation**. Every service starts the same:
 We call on Father, Son, and Spirit—triune God by name.

Invocation: Every church service begins with the Invocation, in which the pastor says, "In the name of the Father and of the Son and of the Holy Spirit." The word "invocation" means "to call upon." When the pastor begins the service in this way, we are calling upon God's name, asking Him to bless our worship.

The pastor also makes the sign of the cross, and each member can do the same. This reminds us of our Baptism, where we were baptized into that same name of God, the Holy Trinity. From the very beginning of the church service, our focus is on our God, who saves us and who is present with us in the Divine Service.

J points us to **Jesus**, who alone can **Justify**.

He takes our sin so we may stand before God's throne on high.

Jesus/Justify: To "justify" is to "declare righteous." Jesus, God's Son, came to earth as a human being in order to make us right with God. Our sin separates us from our holy God, but Jesus lived a perfect life for us, died on the cross for our sins, and rose from the grave to life everlasting. He suffered the punishment for our sins in our place. Because of Jesus' sacrifice for us, God forgives our sins and remembers them no more. Romans 3:23–24 states that "all have sinned and fall short of the glory of God, and are justified by His grace as a gift, through the redemption that is in Christ Jesus." A good way to remember what "justify" means is to say that it is "just as if I" had never sinned. God sees Jesus' perfection when He looks at us. Our own works cannot save us. We are justified only by Jesus.

K
is for the **Kyrie**, a simple, heartfelt plea.
"Lord, have mercy,"so we pray in our liturgy.

Kyrie: "Kyrie" means "Lord." In the divine service, we find a form of the liturgical prayer called "Kyrie eleison." In it we pray, "Lord, have mercy. Christ, have mercy. Lord, have mercy." The Kyrie comes shortly after the Confession and Absolution of sins. In the Kyrie, we are asking God to hear and answer our prayers according to His holy will. The Divine Service may also include short petitions, such as "For the peace from above and for our salvation, let us pray to the Lord," to which the response is "Lord, have mercy." The use of the Kyrie in liturgical worship dates to the first century, but even throughout the Bible, there are many examples of people crying to the Lord for mercy.

The Lord's Prayer is our letter

L,

and here we are assured

That when we pray these words of Christ, before our God we're heard.

Our Father who art in heaven, hallowed be Thy name, Thy kingdom come, Thy will be done on earth as it is in heaven; give us this day our daily bread; and forgive us our trespasses as we forgive those who trespass against us; and lead us not into temptation, but deliver us from evil. For thine is the kingdom and the power and the glory forever and ever. Amen

Lord's Prayer: The Lord's Prayer is one of the Six Chief Parts in the catechism. It is so named because it was first given by Jesus to His followers to pray (see Luke 11:1–4). There are seven "petitions," or requests, in the Lord's Prayer, as well as an introduction and a conclusion. Of the seven petitions, only one asks God for physical blessings ("give us this day our daily bread"). The others are spiritual requests. Martin Luther explains each of the petitions in more detail in the Small Catechism, and confirmands are expected to memorize these meanings. The Lord's Prayer is prayed aloud by the entire congregation in every Lutheran worship service.

Martin **Luther** is our

M,

a man by God
made bold.

"Here I stand,"
his famous vow,
"God's teachings
I do hold."

Martin Luther: Born in 1483, Luther has had a tremendous impact on the history of Christianity. He started out as a Roman Catholic monk but soon realized the teachings of that church body had become so burdened by man-made rules that there was little room for the Gospel. He viewed God as harsh and punishing until he started studying the Bible himself. There, he discovered the truth that God forgives sin and loves us. Luther wanted to reform the religious teachings of the church of his day to bring this comfort to the people and to reverse the abuses that had crept into the church's teaching. He made his Ninety-Five Theses (his list of statements) public on October 31, 1517. For the rest of his life, Luther worked hard to bring the pure Gospel to the people. He translated the Bible into German so the people in his country could read it for themselves, and he wrote the Small Catechism and other books to explain the doctrines of Holy Scripture. He was told many times to recant, or deny and withdraw, his teachings. He replied that unless he was convinced by Scripture, he would not change his beliefs. Eventually he was excommunicated, or removed, from the Roman Catholic Church. But Luther always remained a devout believer in Jesus. He died in 1546.

N is for the **Nicene Creed**. Jesus is God's Son.
This creed explains that we believe in God, the Three-in-One.

Nicene Creed: The Nicene Creed is so named because this statement of belief was adopted in Nicaea in the year 325. It was the church's response to false teachings about Jesus. These false teachings denied the deity, or divinity, of Christ. A man named Arius was teaching that Jesus was a created being, and therefore slightly less than the Father. This heresy, or false teaching about God, threatened people's understanding of the Trinity and had the potential to lead people away from the Christian faith. The council that convened at Nicaea reaffirmed the biblical teaching of the Trinity: one God in three equal persons. Jesus is rightly confessed as "God of God, Light of Light, very God of very God, begotten, not made, being of one substance with the Father." There is no question that Jesus is indeed God. Lutherans often confess the Nicene Creed together in church during services with Holy Communion.

The **Office of the Keys** is

O.

We have this guarantee

That pastors pardon all our sins by Christ's authority. ∎

Office of the Keys: Every Divine Service includes Confession and Absolution, when we confess our sins and are assured by the pastor that God forgives our sins through Jesus. We use the term "Office of the Keys" for this special authority given to pastors to forgive sins in Christ's stead, or on His behalf. It is called this because pastors have the responsibility given to them by Christ, through the call at his church, to unlock the gates of heaven to penitent sinners through forgiveness, but to withhold forgiveness from those who do not repent. To the unrepentant, the gates of heaven remain locked. This is done in accordance with Jesus' command to His disciples in John 20:23: "If you forgive the sins of any, they are forgiven them; if you withhold forgiveness from any, it is withheld."

P
is for our
Pastors.
These men by
God are sent

To carry
out the
ministry of
Word and
Sacrament.

Pastors: Pastors are a vital part of the church's ministry. These men traditionally go through four years of training at a seminary before they are called and ordained into the Office of the Holy Ministry. A Lutheran pastor is called by a congregation to be their shepherd, a responsibility not to be taken lightly. Pastors are charged with the spiritual care of those in their congregation. Spiritual care includes preaching and teaching, leading worship, officiating at weddings and funerals, and praying with and for the members of his congregation and community. Lutheran pastors have a "Word and Sacrament ministry," which means they are to boldly preach the truths of God's Word and to administer the Sacraments of Baptism and Holy Communion. When a pastor is ordained into the ministry or is installed at a particular congregation, he vows to remain faithful to the teachings of the Bible and to the Lutheran Confessions. These Confessions express Lutheran doctrine as found in the Word of God. Those who are members of a congregation should pray regularly for their pastor, asking God to help him carry out the duties of his office faithfully and joyfully.

Q

's a famous **Question** that we as Lutherans know. "What does this mean?" we ask in faith that we in truth may grow.

Question: "What does this mean?" It's a question every Lutheran knows well after studying the catechism. Martin Luther used this question frequently to further explain each of the Ten Commandments, the three Articles of the Apostles' Creed, and the seven Petitions of the Lord's Prayer. Confirmands are required to memorize these meanings during their formal instruction, and parents are strongly encouraged to teach them to their children from early on. Luther's hope was that all Christians would know the catechism well and use it as a tool for studying and understanding the Bible. This is evidenced by Luther's introduction to the Six Chief Parts of the Small Catechism: "As the head of the family should teach it in a simple way to his household."

R is **Reformation**, where we commemorate
Luther's work to spread the Gospel. That's cause to celebrate!

Reformation: Lutherans celebrate Reformation Day on October 31 and observe the festival in church on the final Sunday of October. On October 31, 1517, Martin Luther made his Ninety-Five Theses public by nailing them to the door of the church in Wittenberg, Germany. (In Luther's time, this was the common way for making announcements and for inviting people to respond.) His hope was to begin a discussion about religious practices of the Roman Catholic Church of his day. Many of the Ninety-Five Theses address the subject of indulgences, pieces of paper sold to reduce people's time in purgatory (a false teaching that there is an "in-between" state between heaven and hell after death). Luther saw that the Roman Catholic Church was harming people by charging them large amounts of money to buy their way into heaven. This practice hurt people financially, but more important, it was spiritually dangerous. Indulgences gave the false hope that we can contribute to our salvation, while the Bible says that we can never buy salvation or earn it on our own. Salvation comes by God's grace alone through faith alone in Jesus Christ. The Ninety-Five Theses were merely a starting point for Luther's own understanding of the Bible. He continued to study the Bible in depth and realized many other errors that had crept into the church's teachings and practice. On Reformation Day, we remember Luther's efforts to return the Christian Church of his day to true biblical teaching. Luther never intended to start his own denomination. Instead, as Reformation Day indicates, he wished to reform, or correct, the unbiblical teachings of Rome.

Communion is a **Sacrament**, our

S,

and we believe That we Christ's body and His blood with bread and wine receive.

Sacrament of the Altar: Holy Communion is also called the "Lord's Supper" or the "Sacrament of the Altar." In this Sacrament, we receive the true body and blood of Jesus Christ under the bread and wine. This teaching is clear in the Bible, for Jesus tells His disciples, "Take, eat; this is My body, which is given for you. . . . Drink of it, all of you, this cup is the new testament in My blood, which is shed for you for the forgiveness of sins." Jesus' institution, or beginning, of the Lord's Supper is found in three of the four Gospel accounts: Matthew 26, Mark 14, and Luke 22, as well as in 1 Corinthians 11. In Holy Communion, we receive Christ's body and blood to strengthen us in our Christian walk as we are assured of our forgiveness through Jesus.

The **Ten Commandments** is our **T** and here we plainly see
Our need for Christ, for only He has kept them perfectly.

Ten Commandments: The Ten Commandments—what Christians call God's Law or, simply, the Law—form the first of the Six Chief Parts of the catechism. God gave the Commandments to Moses on Mount Sinai. They are found in Exodus 20 and Deuteronomy 5. Although God commands His people to obey them, the fact is that none of us can ever obey them perfectly, nor can we be saved by our obedience to God. God demands perfection, and while we should certainly strive to keep the Commandments, we are also reminded of how sinful we are when we examine our actions in light of them. The Law has three purposes. It acts as a curb to keep our sinful actions in check, a guide to show us how we should live, and most important, a mirror in which we see reflected back at us our sin and need for a Savior. Ultimately, the Law points us to Jesus, who alone was without sin.

U

is for the **Unity** we in our creed confess.
With saints in heaven and saints on earth, as one our God we bless.

Unity: All Christians are part of what is called the "invisible Church," which includes all people throughout the world who believe in Jesus as their Savior. Only God knows this true number, since He alone can see what is in a person's heart. As Christians, we are united not only with other Christians here on earth, but also with the saints in heaven—believers who have died and have been taken to heaven. All who confess Jesus as Lord are united in this "one holy Christian and apostolic Church," as we confess in the Nicene Creed. In the Proper Preface of the Communion liturgy, the pastor says, "Therefore, with angels and archangels, and with all the company of heaven, we laud and magnify Your glorious name, evermore praising You . . ." The truth is that when we praise God, we are united with all fellow Christians, those in heaven and those on earth, in all places and all times. We are worshiping with saints and angels, united in our purpose of praising our Creator and Redeemer!

V

V is for the **Vestments** Lutheran pastors wear each week. They're worn with a robe of white, for it's God's Word they speak.

Vestments: Why do pastors wear robes and clerical collars? To point to Christ! There are different colors for the different seasons of the Church Year. The stole is worn around the neck and shoulders so it hangs down both sides in front, much as a yoke would be worn on an ox. This shows that pastors are "yoked," or bound, to the truths of Scripture and are to preach only what the Bible teaches. Some pastors choose to wear a chasuble, which is similar to a cape, over the alb, or robe. It is also in the liturgical color of the season and shows they are cloaked in Christ. No matter what vestments the pastor wears, we are reminded that our pastors are sent by Christ Himself to bring His Word to us.

W is for the **Word** of God. The Bible clearly shows
That everyone has sinned. That's why Jesus died and rose. ■

Word of God: The Bible is called the "Word of God" because that's exactly what it is—God's Word to us. We believe that the Bible is inspired, literally "God-breathed." The Holy Spirit gave the biblical writers the message and the very words they were to write. We can be sure that the Bible is God's Word and not man's own invention. There are 66 books in the Bible—39 in the Old Testament (the time before Christ) and 27 books in the New Testament (the time of Christ and the period after His death and resurrection). In both the Old and New Testaments, there are two major themes that can be found throughout: Law and Gospel. The Law gives rules (Commandments) that God commands us to follow. The Law demands perfection, and it brings us to the

sober realization that we are naturally sinful and can never be perfect. Because we cannot obey the Law to God's expectation and because we cannot make up for our sin, we are condemned; we are worthy only of God's eternal judgment. But God's Word tells us that there is hope for us. It is the Gospel of Jesus Christ that shows us that we don't have to save ourselves. Jesus has done this for us. He took our punishment on Himself, and we are therefore forgiven. He suffered, died, and rose for us, earning heaven for those who believe in Him as Redeemer and Savior. This is the theme of the entire Bible. Through the Bible's historical accounts, prophecies, psalms, and epistles (letters), God's Word points us always to Jesus and what He did for us.

X

X is in the great **eXchange**. Christ Jesus took our sin
And gives us His own righteousness so we are pure within.

eXchange: The heart of the Christian faith is the "great exchange." Jesus, who was sinless, took our sin upon Himself when He died on the cross. In exchange, He gave us His righteousness. Jesus literally exchanged places with us. When God the Father looked at Jesus on the cross, He saw and punished all the sin of the world. Jesus died for that sin. He went to hell. As we confess in the creeds, we know that Jesus was victorious over sin—He rose from death to live eternally in heaven.

Through hearing the Gospel or through our Baptism, the Holy Spirit gave us faith to believe that Jesus' death on the cross bought our forgiveness. Now when God the Father looks at us, He sees that we are clothed in Jesus' perfection. It is as if we've never sinned. Paul says it this way: "For our sake He made Him to be sin who knew no sin, so that in Him we might become the righteousness of God" (2 Corinthians 5:21). Praise be to God for this amazing truth!

Y

is for our **Youth**, and when they are confirmed,

They state their faith and vow that they'll hold fast to what they've learned.

Youth: As Christians, we realize the importance of training up the next generation to be faithful followers of Christ. Christian education begins in the home with parents modeling a prayer life. Many Lutheran congregations support Christian day schools, where children are taught about Jesus throughout the typical school day. Also, beginning with Sunday School for children ages preschool and up, we teach our children biblical accounts and encourage them to memorize Bible verses. In middle school or junior high, students take a more structured approach to their instruction by studying the catechism and Lutheran doctrines in confirmation class. During this time, students memorize the Six Chief Parts, complete homework, and take tests to reinforce what Lutherans

believe. At the end of their formal instruction, they have the Rite of Confirmation. This is a service in which the confirmands stand before the congregation, confirm their beliefs, and promise to continue in the faith and the teachings of the Lutheran Church. They are accepted as communicant members of the church and are strongly encouraged to remain active in their congregations. Most churches have a high school youth group that meets on Sunday mornings for Bible class and arranges social activities for the members. There are also youth gatherings on larger levels, such as Higher Things and the National Youth Gathering, which takes place every three years. These are all opportunities for our youth to continue to grow in knowledge of the Bible and to be strengthened in their Christian walk.

Z points us to **Zion**, our home in heav'n above.

We'll live with Christ forever there because of His great love.

Zion: The name Zion first occurs in the Old Testament account of King David's capture of the city of Jerusalem from the Jebusites (2 Samuel 5:6–10). Because of its mountaintop location and its fortifications, the city was quite a stronghold. The Jebusites were confident that David could never defeat them and take their city. But with God's help, David won a great victory and took Jerusalem as his own capital city. Jerusalem became known as the City of David. The temple was built here, and "Zion" became synonymous with the Lord's dwelling among His people. Already in the Psalms, Zion is considered a holy place. Psalm 50:2 says, "Out of Zion, the perfection of beauty, God shines forth." And Psalm 99:2 claims, "The LORD is great in Zion; He is exalted over all the peoples." Because of this association with God dwelling on high (on the mount), the Bible refers to heaven as Zion. Revelation 14, a clear picture of the Lamb (Jesus) in heaven, states in verse 1, "Behold, on Mount Zion stood the Lamb." Our future in heaven is certain, thanks to our Savior. We pray, as does the apostle John in Revelation 22:20, "Amen. Come, Lord Jesus!"

A Apostles' Creed

B Baptism

C Catechism

D Doctrine

E Evangelism

F Faith Alone

G God

H Hymnals

I Invocation

J Jesus/Justify

K Kyrie

L Lord's Prayer

M Martin Luther

N Nicene Creed

O Office of the Keys

P Pastors

Q Question

R Reformation

S Sacrament of the Altar

T Ten Commandments

U Unity

V Vestments

W Word of God

X eXchange

Y Youth

Z Zion